ISBN 978-0-9768680-2-6

Published in the United States of America by

burningbush creation
2114 Queen Ave North
Minneapolis, MN 55411-2435

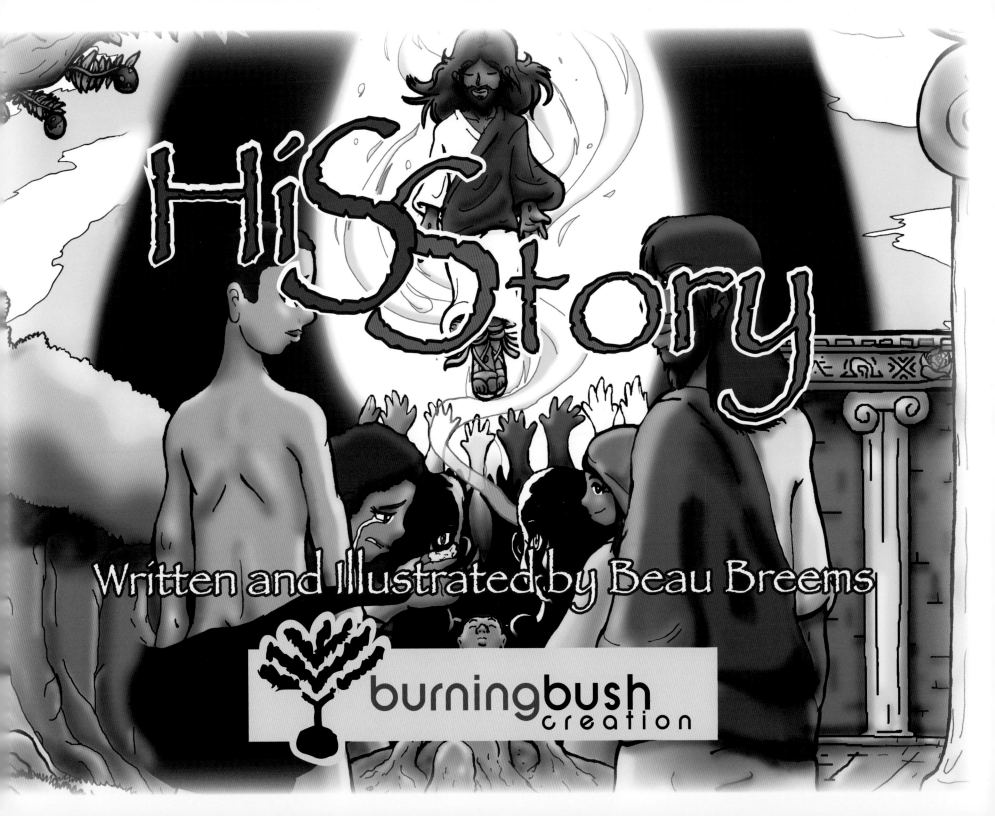

Acknowledgements

This book is the result of a request made by two ladies in my church, Liz Pope and Joyce Roufs, who were taking a mission trip to Africa in the fall of 2004. (I was only 18 years old then!) God had impressed upon them to ask me to make something for them that they could take with them for the children and adults that they would be ministering to. So, after some prayer and some studying, I began. Several months later, a very early version of this book was made, and only three copies were printed. Two for the ladies, and one for myself to keep. And that would have been the end.

But a youth leader in my church, Ron McConico, felt that this book was meant for more, and after a conference addressing Urban Ministry, and the reactions many people had towards the book, he knew that God wanted him to drop everything and get this book published. And now, after a lot of work, time, and prayer, you have this product before you! This is truly a book that was taken to where it is through God's amazing providence.

I'd like to thank all the people who contributed financially to the book, and those who stood in prayer for the book. Also, thanks goes to MGB Printing for taking the leap of faith to invest in this project and print it. You can see more of their products at MGBprinting.com. I'd also like to thank my team members of Burning Bush Creation; My friend Brandon McCall, my Mentor Nick Kmoch, and my discipler Ron McConico, all of whom's efforts in this endeavor were indispensable. And of course, all the thanks and glory truly goes to God, who not only started this project and saw it through, but was the director of the true events described in this book. From creation to resurrection, God is truly worthy of all the glory, honor, and praise.

This book is dedicated to the people of Africa... and now the world.

CHAPTER 1: CREATION

Have you ever wondered how the world came to be?
Well, there is an answer. The God of the universe told us in His own words how He created the world. Throughout history, there have been people that God has chosen to speak to, and He did so through His Spirit. Those people wrote down what God was saying in the Bible. God said that in the beginning He created the heavens and the earth.

On the first day of creation, He made the earth without form and the heavens without stars. But He said, "Let there be light," and there was light. And He called the light "day", and He separated it from the darkness, which He called "night". On the second day, He separated the waters from below from the waters above, and made the dry land. On the third day, He filled the land with grass, herbs, fruit, and trees, each after their own kind.

2

On the fourth day, God created the sun, moon, and stars,
putting them in place for seasons, days, and years. On the
fifth day, God created the water-dwelling creatures and the
winged creatures, each after their own kind. On the sixth day,
God created the earth creatures~creeping things and walking
things, all after their own kind. He told all of earth's creatures
to be fruitful and to multiply.

On the sixth day, God also created the first man, Adam, from the dust of the ground. God gave Adam rule over the earth and all creatures. God gave them all the grass, fruit, and herbs to eat. On the seventh day, God rested from His work of creation and saw that everything was good.

God put Adam in a garden called Eden, and then brought all of the animals to Adam.

Adam named them all, but he could not find a partner that was like him among the animals.

Since Adam did not have a
partner like him, God
created a helper from
Adam's rib.

She was called woman,
since she came from man,
and Adam named her Eve,
the first of all women.

CHAPTER 2: THE FALL

God allowed Adam and Eve to eat any fruit they chose in the Garden of Eden, but told them not to eat from the tree of the knowledge of good and evil.

God warned them that if they did, they would surely die.

However, the enemy of God, Satan, entered the body of a serpent, and told Eve that they would not die if they ate fruit from the tree of the knowledge of good and evil. Satan had put doubt into the heart of humans, fooling them into disobeying God.

"Your eyes will be opened!" Satan told her. "You will be like God! You will not die."

So Eve collected some of the fruit for herself and her husband to eat. She didn't know that she had been tricked.

So Adam and Eve disobeyed God, their creator and provider, by eating fruit from the tree of the knowledge of good and evil. Their eyes were suddenly opened as they ate the fruit, and they realized what a terrible mistake they had made.

Adam and Eve realized that they were naked and were ashamed, so they tried to hide from each other and cover themselves with leaves. Soon, God came walking through the garden, and Adam and Eve hid from Him.

God soon found them. He questioned them and gave them punishments for their disobedience. The serpent was cursed to slither the ground forever, man was forced to work the earth for food, and women now had great pain in childbirth.

Not only were these punishments laid on them for their disobedience, but they were also sent out from the Garden of Eden. This was the first time mankind had disobeyed God.

But this was only the beginning.

Not only were Adam and Eve cursed, but also we, their children, and the entire world was cursed. Sin, which had now entered the world, is the result of our disobedience to God. Sin separates us from God, and we all sin, just as our father Adam did by disobeying God. We are born with sin, as if it were a disease, inherited from our parents. Because of this, people and animals die, and our very character is corrupted into disobeying God. Animals eat animals. Brothers kill brothers. Friends betray friends. Nations enslave nations. Some prayed for help.

13

CHAPTER 3: HOPE

But God still loved the world. He wanted everyone to love Him, and serve Him. So God made a way for them to be forgiven. The Jewish people, once slaves to Egypt, were freed by God through miraculous feats. God gave them His instructions for living, the Law, and a land to live in. Burnt sacrifices of animals were offered so God would forgive their sins; the shedding of innocent blood. But though the Law taught them how to live right, the people still could not overcome their sin. So God promised a savior, to save the entire world from sin!

Time continued, and so did the death and decay caused by sin. Then, about two thousand years ago, a virgin gave birth to a son. This was just what was said by the Jewish prophets; those who heard God's words and made them known. God had given this virgin, Mary, a son. Because this son had no human father, he did not inherit sin. His name was Jesus, and he spent his younger years studying the Jewish scriptures and working as a carpenter. He lived a sinless life, and knew that God had sent him with a mission.

A relative of Jesus, John the Baptist, was baptizing people in these times, putting them underwater and lifting them out. This was a sign of a new life and was done to show that this person was going to follow God. Many thought that John was the savior, the 'Messiah'. But he was not. He was preparing the way for the Messiah.

When Jesus came to be baptized by John, the Holy Spirit of God came down from heaven upon him like a dove, and God's voice was heard from heaven, saying, "This is my beloved Son" Jesus was the promised Messiah, who would save the world from sin.

After his baptism, Jesus went into the desert, fasting and praying for forty days and forty nights.

Satan, the one who had tricked Adam and Eve, tempted Jesus three times, trying to make him misuse the power he had been given by God.

But Jesus stood against Satan and overcame the temptations.

Where Adam and Eve had failed the battle, Jesus had won.

Jesus was sinless!

Jesus then began to travel throughout the land of Judea, preaching to the Jewish people that God's kingdom was near. Many people followed him and Jesus made students or 'disciples', out of normal people, like fisherman. Jesus' disciples learned closely from him and became his friends.

Jesus also did miracles, doing things that no one could ever do. He healed people of sickness and handicaps, like leprosy and blindness. He even had power over nature! He walked on water, and told plants to wither. Jesus did not prove himself by his words alone, but proved by his actions that he was the Messiah.

Jesus gave sight to the blind, made the lame to walk, multiplied enough to feed thousands from a few pieces of food, and even raised the dead. People flocked to him for healing. Even those who were not Jewish begged for his healing touch. Jesus also forgave sins, something that only God could do. He proved through his actions that he was not just God's son, but God himself! God had come to save the world!

22

Jesus was also a great teacher. He taught parables to the people and to his disciples, showing them spiritual truths about how to live, and about himself. He showed them how he and his Father were one, but separate; one God in two persons, the Father and the Son.

CHAPTER 4: HIS LAST WEEK

But many of the Jewish religious leaders of the day believed that Jesus was lying and none hated his teachings more than the Pharisees. They followed the Law strictly, and would not believe Jesus, even though he did many great miracles right in front of their eyes. They plotted against Jesus.

But Jesus knew what his purpose on earth was. After years of teaching and doing miracles, he knew his time on the planet was near an end. He would have to go to the city of Jerusalem to fulfill God's promise to the world. The Messiah would save us; but he would do it at a great cost.

Jesus rode into Jerusalem on a donkey, and his followers and fans celebrated! They laid palm branches at his feet and said, "Blessed is he who comes in the name of the Lord!" They believed Jesus had come to save them from the ones that had taken over Judea, the Romans. But Jesus would save all people from sin.

Jesus spent his final week in Jerusalem teaching that it was only through him that the people's sins could be forgiven. He taught that he was the Messiah, and put to rest every argument of the Pharisees. They plotted to kill Jesus during the Jewish festival that was taking place in Jerusalem that week.

But God's enemy Satan had not given up in trying to stop Jesus' work. He entered one of Jesus' disciples, Judas Iscariot, and through Judas betrayed Jesus to the Pharisees. The Pharisees paid Judas to lead them to Jesus so they could arrest, accuse, and judge Jesus during the festival.

On the night he was betrayed, Jesus had one last meal with his disciples. He told them that he would suffer and die for the whole world's sins, but then rise again. He said his body would be broken like bread, and his blood poured out like wine. He would be a sacrifice to pay the price of sin that the world owed to God.

Jesus then taught them a final lesson in serving by washing their feet. He humbled himself before them, showing by his actions and words that they were to love God with all of their heart, mind, strength and soul, and to love everyone as they love themselves. They were to serve each other like he was serving them.

They then went to the garden called Gethsemane, and Jesus prayed late into the night. Jesus didn't want to die, but he humbled himself to do what God wanted. Jesus, the sinless one, would take the world's sin upon himself. He was innocent, but would do it out of love for God and for everyone on the entire earth.

CHAPTER 5: BETRAYAL

Late in the night Judas found Jesus, and was leading the Roman guards that had been sent by the Pharisees to arrest Jesus. Judas was broken inside because of his betrayal, and he, along with the rest of Jesus' disciples, fled. Jesus was now completely alone. But Jesus was ready to finish his Father's work.

Jesus was brought before the Jewish leaders, was judged, and thrown in jail. He was then put on trial before the Roman Governor in Jerusalem, Pontius Pilate. He was to be beaten thirty-nine times with whips. The Messiah was said to be king of the Jewish people- so the Romans placed a crown of thorns on his head to make fun of him. Jesus was then sentenced to death.

Jesus was forced to carry the cross that he would later hang on. The people mocked and spit on him. But they didn't know what they were doing.

They didn't understand that they were killing God's only son.

Nails were driven through Jesus' hands and feet, and a sign was hung over his head saying that this was the king of the Jewish people. He was hung between two criminals who were also being put to death. One cursed Jesus, but the other knew that Jesus was innocent. His sins were forgiven because of his faith in Jesus.

All of the sins of the people of the world were put on Jesus as he hung on the cross. By shedding his innocent blood, Jesus paid the price for sin on our behalf. As Adam had sinned in the beginning, so Jesus did not sin in the end. But God sacrificed His only son for the sins of the world, your sins and mine. God did all of this for you because even though you've sinned against Him He still loves you, and wants you to be with Him in this life and in the next. A terrible darkness swept over the land as Jesus died, and the earth shook. The people finally realized- they had killed the Messiah.

CHAPTER 6: RESURRECTION

Jesus was then buried in a tomb, and Roman guards were posted outside the tomb to protect it from thieves. But three days later, some women who had followed Jesus came to the tomb to cover his body with spices. But when they came upon the tomb early in the morning, something amazing had happened.

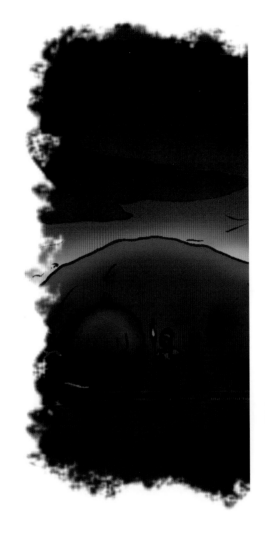

Angels had come and removed the stone door from the tomb and had caused the guards to faint. The women went into the tomb and found Jesus' body was gone, but his grave clothes laying as if they had never been removed. The angels inside told the women that Jesus had risen from the dead!

Jesus later appeared to the women alive and then appeared to his disciples. He still had the holes that had been pierced into his body. He was the same Jesus, but he had risen from the dead. Jesus appeared to his disciples and many others over the course of forty days, proving that it was through faith in him alone that God would forgive a person.

Jesus showed them from the Jewish scriptures how he was God's sacrifice, and that he had fulfilled all of the things spoken about him from God through the Jewish prophets. From creation to resurrection, Jesus' sacrifice was always God's plan. Years later, all of these things and more would be recorded in the Bible.

After forty days, Jesus then rose to heaven in the company of his disciples. Jesus promised that one day he will return to earth as king to judge everyone, even those who believe in him. Those who do not believe in him will be forever separated from God in hell, because they did not accept God's free gift of forgiveness in faith.

But what about today? Though we all will die someday because of our sinful nature, we can be forgiven by giving our life in faith to Jesus. When we die, we will then go to heaven, God's kingdom. We will live with Him forever if we believe in Jesus' sacrifice, and our need for forgiveness.

God wants us to be with Him and trust Him. He wants us to use our earthly lives to tell others about His free gift of forgiveness, just like Jesus did. This is not just a story- this is real **HiStory** and you can accept God's forgiveness right now by confessing your sinfulness to God and asking for forgiveness through Jesus. He's waiting.

The Bible says...

"That if you confess with your mouth, 'Jesus is Lord', and believe in your heart that God raised Him from the dead, you will be saved."

Romans 10:9

Pray this prayer now:

Dear Lord Jesus
I know that I am a sinner and need your forgiveness. I believe that you died for my sins. I want to turn away from my sins. Please come into my heart and my life and forgive me. I want to trust and follow you as my Lord and Savior. In your name I pray
Amen

If you've just prayed this prayer and meant it with all of your heart, congratulations! God has forgiven you, as He's promised- you are part of His family. To learn more about a relationship with Jesus Christ call 1-888-NeedHim. You can also learn more at www.needhim.com   Welcome home.

Now that you've read HisStory, what's your story?

We'd love to hear from you! Tell us how Jesus has affected your life!

www.hisstory.biz/yourstory.htm

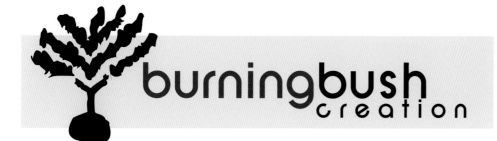

ORDER FORM

Individual Prints

We are making the art in this book available to special order. You may order the prints in small, medium, or large.

- Small prints are 8x10

- Medium prints are 11x17

- Large prints are 16x22

- They may be ordered framed or unframed

"Dust"

Price List

Small	Unframed	$11.95
	Framed	$34.95
Medium	Unframed	$23.95
	Framed	$64.95
Large	Unframed	$35.95
	Framed	$94.95

Framed print will be framed in oak with a complimentary mat.

Shipping for prints by FedX	Unframed	$8.00
	Framed	$25.00

"His Story" Hard Cover	$19.95
"His Story" Soft Cover	$14.95
"La Gran Historia" Hard Cover	$19.95
"La Gran Historia" Soft Cover	$14.95
"His Story" Limited Edition	$200.00

Comes with
- A copy of the original artwork used in His Story
- Single custom hand drawn page.
    Every book will be 1 of 1

Prices subject to change without notice. For current prices, check our website www. burningbushcreation.com

Order Form

Item#	Page#	Qty.	Price	Subtotal

Order total: _____
Tax: _____
Shipping: _____
Total: _____

Name: _____

Address: _____
_____
_____

Phone: _____ E-mail: _____

Method of Payment
- ☐ Cash ☐ Check
- ☐ Visa ☐ MasterCard
- ☐ Discover ☐ American Express

Credit Card # _____

Exp. Date   Signature

_____

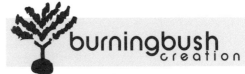

2114 Queen Ave North
Minneapolis, MN 55411-2435

Phone: 612-529-0198
Fax: 612-529-0199
E-mail: orders@burningbushcreation.com